Foreword: An American Artist

Faith and Harmony is not just another coloring book but a treasure and gift from one of today's most inspiring artists and craftsmen who brings his passion for art, history, family, and country to every single page.

I had the great privilege of working with Jim Shore many years ago during my time as an executive in the gift industry. Jim introduced me to a world of design and a creative process that continues to inspire me to this day. His design style and down-to-earth personality have inspired millions of people around the world for many years, but more importantly taught us all how to celebrate the rich design heritage found in the world of quilting and folk art. As an artist and designer, my appreciation for Jim's ability to celebrate the past while introducing a new, unique, and inspiring art style goes beyond words.

As a colorist, you will find not only endless hours of inspirational coloring in the pages of *Faith and Harmony* but also an opportunity to celebrate the patterns and motifs rich in quilting and folk-art history. These folk-art themes are all very much alive and celebrated today deep in the heart of Lancaster County, Pennsylvania—the home of Fox Chapel Publishing.

Faith and Harmony is a rare opportunity to follow the hands of a master artisan. As president of Fox Chapel Publishing, I'm grateful to Jim for sharing this amazing portfolio of his designs that can be admired and colored for years to come by all ages. My heartfelt thanks to Jim for sharing his deep passion for history and the people and art that have inspired him over the years.

Fox Chapel Publishing is headquartered in the heart of Amish country in Lancaster County, Pennsylvania. Our company and community have a deep appreciation for Jim's work and his passion for preserving the rich heritage and ethics of a land and people who continue to celebrate the importance of simpler times!

—David Miller
    President, Fox Chapel Publishing
    Mount Joy, Pennsylvania

You will find Amish quilts for sale throughout Pennsylvania Dutch country. This quilt auction benefitted a local fire company in Lancaster County, where Fox Chapel Publishing is headquartered.

Enjoy Some Uplifting Fun!

T he title of this book means a lot to me. *Faith* and *harmony* are two words that exist at the heart of my life and my art. They don't always come easily; often there's a good deal of "artistic license" involved. But I've found over the years that with some creativity, and a good deal of persistence, both can be achieved!

The *harmony* part of this book's title is inspired by the past. I grew up in rural South Carolina, the son of artistic parents who instilled in me a love for the traditional imagery found in American folk art. There's an innocence, a purity, in the designs found in early American art that we can still see influences of today, particularly in Pennsylvania Dutch art. The art that was created just as the US was forming are masterpieces designed by people driven to create. These artists were otherwise ordinary men and women who found beauty and harmony in an often-hostile environment. It's a tradition I admire and a shared heritage that inspires my own work down to the last detail.

My experience as a struggling artist is a testament to the power of *faith*. I left a career as a mechanical engineer, which meant that I pretty much took a chance on everything to follow my dream. Those were hard times. My wife and I were living in a converted mule shed until things started to change and orders started coming in. Success, as the world defines it, followed. But we'd already found what made us happy. Faith in our dreams and in ourselves. Harmony in our shared life together.

It's my hope that the art in this book conveys messages of positivity to you. As you work on coloring in the wholesome illustrations, I invite you to think on how faith and harmony have enriched your life, or, if you feel you need a little more of one or both, how that can be achieved.

God bless,
Jim Shore

A COLORFUL LIFE

Coloring is something I've done all my life. I remember doing it with my brothers after school, sharing and competing while we laughed together. With 6 kids and 14 grandkids, I've had plenty of experience since, teaching and experimenting with crayons, pencils, watercolors, and the like. And now you could say it's my day job! It's a craft I'm passionate about, and I know I'm not alone. I believe people are driven to create and are drawn to color. It's just the nature of things, part of who we are, a part of being human.

There are hex signs on many barns in Pennsylvania Dutch country. Some folks believe they are symbols of happiness and good fortune.

Something you might see in your grandmother's attic—a painted chest showing the rosemaling technique.

My Work Space

I built my studio myself, so I like to think it's exactly what I need. It's a big, open area that measures about 35' x 50' (11 x 15m). It has tall, gabled ceilings. There's a floor-to-ceiling stone fireplace in the middle of the room that's sort of the centerpiece. And there are 20' (11m) windows on three sides with a kitchen on the fourth side. I have plenty of light and easy access to coffee.

Plentiful coffee helps because it can get pretty busy in here—you might say I like to have a lot going on! At any given moment I can have a dozen or so projects in the works. These run the gamut from bronze casting to stonecutting to glass molding, with characters ranging from Santa Claus to Abraham Lincoln to Tinker Bell. I love it! That variety and activity creates its own sort of energy, a combination of media and design that keeps my mind stimulated. Anyone else might walk in and think it's total chaos, but it's perfect for me, and I always know exactly where everything is . . . mostly.

I think that kind of active, multitasking work environment inspires and influences my art. My work combines elements from different folk-art traditions. I use quilting designs and quilt blocks as a foundation, of course, but I also draw on images from rosemaling, fraktur, and Pennsylvania Dutch designs. I find that mixture of different elements exciting. Creating different combinations keeps the eye moving over the entire work. That movement is what I think makes everything interesting. Creating a visual energy and levels of discovery ensure that there's always something new to see every time you look. That's really what I strive for in every finished design. I have a rule of thumb when I look at one of my pieces. If my eye comes to rest on any one element, no matter how wonderful or exciting that element is, it's wrong and out of place and needs to be changed.

The space where my hardest-working hours and most inspiring artistic moments are spent.

A view of the figurines I've enjoyed creating.

Tools for Coloring

I use a wide range of **colored pencils**. There are, of course, many brands and colors available. I like to use Prismacolor® pencils, which can be purchased at your local craft store or online.

Colored pencils can produce a variety of effects, everything from a very saturated color to subtle color. Changing the pressure and repetition of strokes will get the density you want to achieve.

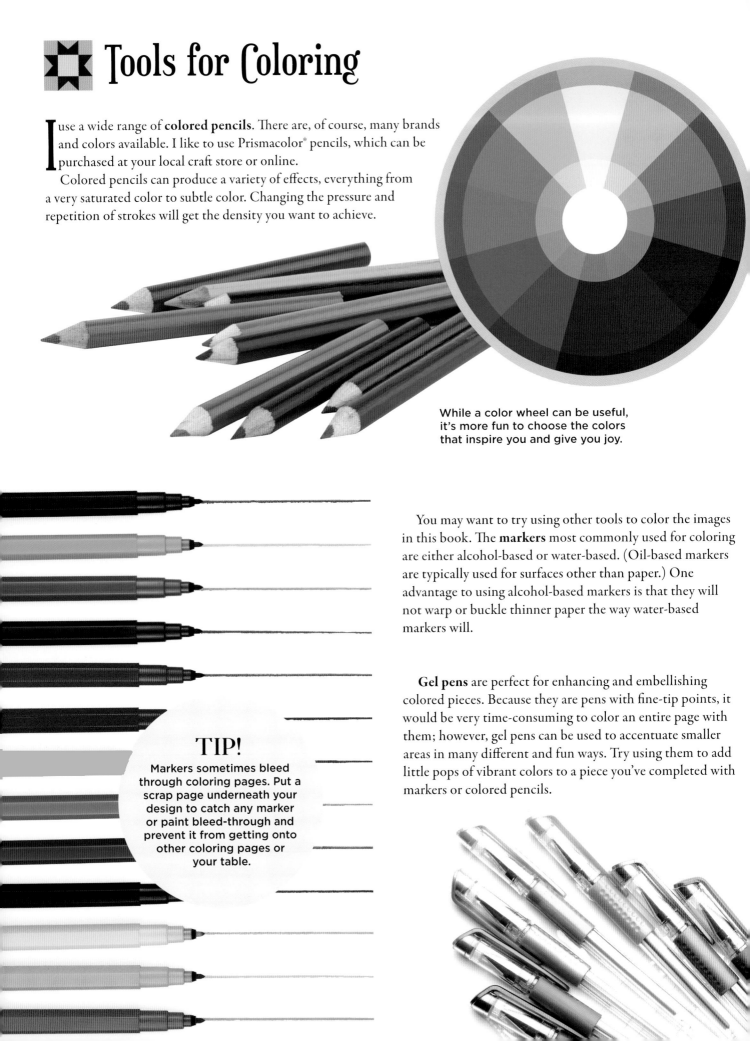

While a color wheel can be useful, it's more fun to choose the colors that inspire you and give you joy.

You may want to try using other tools to color the images in this book. The **markers** most commonly used for coloring are either alcohol-based or water-based. (Oil-based markers are typically used for surfaces other than paper.) One advantage to using alcohol-based markers is that they will not warp or buckle thinner paper the way water-based markers will.

Gel pens are perfect for enhancing and embellishing colored pieces. Because they are pens with fine-tip points, it would be very time-consuming to color an entire page with them; however, gel pens can be used to accentuate smaller areas in many different and fun ways. Try using them to add little pops of vibrant colors to a piece you've completed with markers or colored pencils.

TIP!
Markers sometimes bleed through coloring pages. Put a scrap page underneath your design to catch any marker or paint bleed-through and prevent it from getting onto other coloring pages or your table.

Other Handy Tools

One of my favorite tools is a **stump**. A stump is a hard paper stick that is pointed and shaped similar to a pencil. It's used for blending color in charcoal, pastel, or colored pencil. A stump can be used to manipulate and soften colors once they're applied to the paper.

Other tools I use include the **eraser stick** or battery-operated eraser, and an **eraser shield**. A nice eraser lets you remove any trace of a misplaced line or remove some color to create lighter shades.

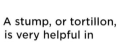

A stump, or tortillon, is very helpful in blending colors.

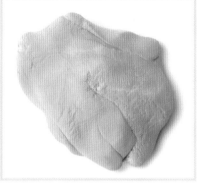

Kneaded eraser

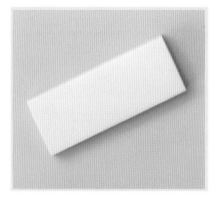

Hard white eraser

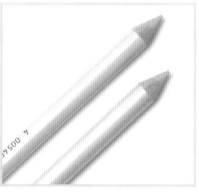

Eraser pencil

Sand eraser

If you've made a mistake with your colored pencil, you have lots of options. A **kneaded eraser** can be formed into any shape to help fit into small areas. Another option is a smooth, hard **white eraser**, which is useful for tough-to-erase colored pencils, and it won't leave behind colored eraser smudges on your paper. You can also get erasers in easy-to-use "mechanical pencil" form (also called eraser sticks) that are in a tube, and you can click out more eraser as you need it. They even make **eraser pencils**! A **sand eraser**, such as this one at left, is perfect for correcting mistakes in colored pencil or even ink. It can also bring back highlights, assist in blending, and bring back the texture of the paper when multiple layers of colored pencil have been applied.

Another great tool is an **eraser shield**. It's used to erase small, precise areas without erasing more than you want. Only what's in the opening gets erased, and the shield protects the areas around it from being erased.

An eraser shield lets you remove very small, specific areas of color.

Techniques

I use several techniques when coloring: shading, highlighting, and blending. Each one helps bring an image to life.

Shading

When shading, you need to decide what tools and method you want to use. There are four general methods. The first creates the most realistic effect.

METHOD 1: Pick two similar shades from the same color family and use them together: a base color (lighter color) and a shade color (darker color).

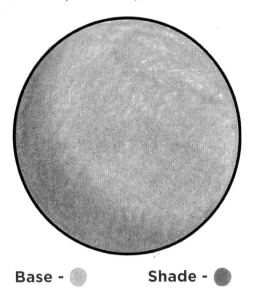

Base - ●   Shade - ●

METHOD 2: Use varying degrees of pressure with a single coloring tool to make the shaded part darker than the rest.

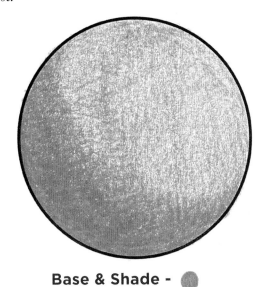

Base & Shade - ●

METHOD 3: Add black or gray where you want shading, or use a totally different color than the one you're using as a base.

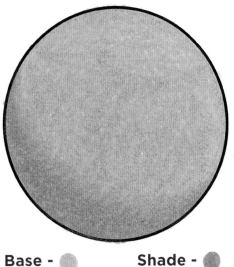

Base - ●   Shade - ●

METHOD 4: Use line techniques like stippling or crosshatching with ink or marker over colored pencil.

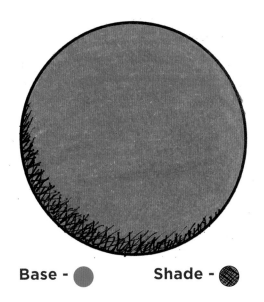

Base - ●   Shade - ●

Highlighting

A simple way to add highlights to your coloring is to use a white gel pen (for strong highlights) or white colored pencil (for subtle highlights). You could also use a kneaded eraser to pick up some of the base color where you would like to place a highlight; this works best with colored pencils. With a little planning, you can simply leave an area uncolored from the beginning to create a highlight.

Gel pen highlight

Colored pencil highlight

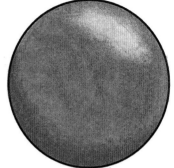
Highlight created by erasing

Blending

Blending allows you to seamlessly combine colors together to create visually stunning art. When blending, you can use any colors or media you want. Try starting with a monochromatic color scheme in one specific medium until you get comfortable with the process. Colored pencils are good tools for beginners to learn blending.

TIP
With colored pencils, tool sharpness and hand pressure make all the difference.

1 Start by laying down the light base color over the entire area you want to blend.

2 Use the dark shade to color lightly from the middle of the base color toward one edge of the shape. As you move farther away from the area of your base shade, begin adding more pressure to your pencil, coloring the area more heavily.

3 Go back with the light base color and color over the base and dark shade areas. Repeat until you've created a nice, even coat of color.

Butterflies are nature's angels.
They remind us what a gift it is to be alive.

—Robyn Nola

NATURE'S DELIGHT

I use angel images in a lot of different ways in my art: to tell a story or celebrate an occasion or specific emotion. Often, they're just an expression of the wonder I find in the world around me, such as the magic of a garden or the beauty of butterfly wings.

And the dove came back to him in the evening, and behold,
in her mouth was a freshly plucked olive leaf.
So Noah knew that the waters had
subsided from the earth.

GENESIS 8:11 (ESV)

FAITH TAKES US THROUGH THE STORM

I've always loved the story of Noah's Ark, and I've used the imagery
and symbols in my art many times over the years. It's a lesson in faith,
hope, and redemption that touches people young and old.

Therefore, since we have been justified through faith,
we have peace with God through our Lord Jesus Christ.

—Romans 5:1 (NIV)

DISTELFINKS

A *distelfink* is a stylized goldfinch that symbolizes happiness and good fortune in the
tradition of the Pennsylvania Dutch. I figure, as in most things, two is better than one!

May the wings of the butterfly kiss the sun
And find your shoulder to light on,
To bring you luck, happiness, and riches
Today, tomorrow, and beyond.

—IRISH BLESSING

BUTTERFLY KISSES

I find inspiration everywhere, from Christmas to angels to flowers and nature to Disney and Peanuts. There's an emotional spark, a connection in what I try to do, and it can take many different forms and cover a lot of different subjects. I try to take the same approach to all of them, devoting the same amount of time and care in designing a large Santa Claus and sleigh as I do a small bird or butterfly.

The reason birds can fly and we can't is simply because they have perfect faith, for to have faith is to have wings.

—J.M. BARRIE

FOREVER TOGETHER

Artists have the reputation for being over-the-top romantics, but I don't think that applies to me! I've found over the years that when it comes to romance, it's best to keep things simple. Chocolates, roses, candlelit dinners; that sort of thing. It's safer that way, and, more importantly, it gets the meaning across more clearly.

Finally, all of you, be like-minded, be sympathetic, love one another, be compassionate and humble.

—1 Peter 3:8 (NIV)

LIGHT OF MY LIFE

Occasionally you just have to keep things simple and straightforward. Images are a great way to convey thoughts and emotions, but sometimes you just have to spell it out!

Humility is the solid foundation of all virtues.

—CONFUCIUS

THREE KINGS

Matthew 2:1–2 (NIV): Magi from the east came to Jerusalem and asked, "Where is the one who has been born king of the Jews? We saw his star when it rose and have come to worship him."

And let the peace of God rule in your hearts,
to which also you were called in one body; and be thankful.

—Colossians 3:15 (NKJV)

MARTHA'S STAR

Both my mother and my grandmother were quilters, so I was born to love it. I've always
admired the skill and imagination behind creating something new and beautiful out of
scraps. To me, it's high art that could be at home in the finest museums around the world.

For it is in giving that we receive.

—St. Francis of Assisi

HEAVEN'S BOUNTY

Fall is a time for color, and Mother Nature isn't timid in how she uses it! She uses orange with purple and red as she mixes in yellow and green. Every now and then she even throws in a surprise, like fuchsia. I love those unexpected combinations, and I love to use them in my art.

Angels have no philosophy but love.

—Terri Guillemets

ANGEL OF PEACE

I don't mind saying that my angels reflect the beauty and love I see in the women in my life. With my wife Jan, our five daughters, and an ever-growing number of granddaughters, I have no shortage of inspiration.

For nothing will be impossible with God.

—LUKE 1:37 (ESV)

FLOCK OF FESTIVE FRIENDS

When I first proposed a collection of snowmen designs, people laughed
and asked, "How can you do that in your style? Snowmen are just three
plain white balls." Thirty years later, I think I've made my point.

Peacemakers who sow in peace
reap a harvest of righteousness.

—James 3:18 (NIV)

PEACE IN THE VALLEY

Perspective can be a tricky thing in folk art. Often, it's more or less ignored! The result can be charming . . . that flat, disproportional look that draws you in precisely because the perspective is off. I use that in my art, along with a more realistic approach to create levels of interest. I love that combination.

A smile is the universal welcome.

—Max Eastman

WELCOME BASKET

Quilt patterns aren't just something I use for decoration, they're also part of
the narrative in my art. I use them to advance the story, to add depth and
nuance. This "grandmother's flower basket" is an excellent example.

It's not how much we give
but how much love we put into giving.

—MOTHER TERESA

ALL HEAVEN'S GLORY

Gardens are a passion of mine. I love the idea of planting, nurturing, and creating a space
that excites the senses. It doesn't matter if it's an acre on a rolling estate or a window
box on an upstairs apartment, there's always something magical about a garden.

Lord bless
this meal ⋄ this home
♡ this family ♡

Time spent in prayer is never wasted.

—FRANCIS FENELON

ALL GOOD GIFTS

I originally created this angel as a Thanksgiving design, using fall colors with
a lot of orange, gold, and purple. The more I look at it, however, the more
I like it as an everyday piece, a prayer for any time, any season.

Turn from evil and do good; seek peace and pursue it.

—PSALM 34:14 (NIV)

SOMETHING TO CROW ABOUT

I got my start as an artist drawing roosters. My mother loved them, so when I
was a kid, I would always draw her a rooster picture on special occasions, like
Mother's Day or her birthday. The hugs and kisses I got in return were the
perfect positive reinforcement–I've been a rooster artist ever since!

A Child is Born

For God so loved the world
that he gave his one and only Son,
that whoever believes in him
shall not perish but have eternal life.

—John 3:16 (NIV)

THE BEGINNING

There's a timeless story at the heart of Christmas: a story of birth, faith, healing,
growth, love, and, finally, redemption. As an artist, it's the most compelling story
I can work on, one that's always inspirational and one I never tire of.

And thus you shall greet him:
"Peace be to you, and peace be to your house,
and peace be to all that you have."

—1 Samuel 25:6 (ESV)

SUMMER RESTORES THE SOUL

Typically, the faces depicted in folk art are more or less expressionless. It's a style I love and an artistic tradition I respect and admire, but, in my work, I like my faces to be more realistic. I like to use them to express emotion and create a connection with the person viewing my art.

To forgive is the highest, most beautiful form of love.
In return, you will receive untold peace and happiness.

—Robert Muller

LIVE IN HARMONY

This illustration reminds me of Isaiah 11:6 (NIV): The wolf will live with
the lamb, the leopard will lie down with the goat, the calf and the lion
and the yearling together; and a little child will lead them.

Humble yourselves before the Lord,
and he will lift you up.

—JAMES 4:10 (NIV)

ROUND ANGEL

No matter what else I have going on, whether I'm working on five projects or twenty, I'm always working on an angel. Angels are a staple in my art, and over the years I must have created thousands. It's a subject I love, an image that keeps inspiring, and an emotional touchstone I'm able to use in a lot of different ways.

So that your faith might not rest in the wisdom of men but in the power of God.

—1 Corinthians 2:5 (ESV)

HOME IN THE COUNTRY

Some people call my studio "controlled chaos." I confess that's more or less true, except for the "controlled" part. I like to have a lot going on, so at any given moment, I might have a dozen or so projects in the works. A simple image like a hen on her nest can help ground me. Of course, it can't be too simple!

For every house is built by someone,
but God is the builder of everything.

—Hebrews 3:4 (NIV)

HOME IS WHERE THE HEART IS

My wife Jan and I got married in an old white two-story house on
the outskirts of our town. It was where we lived and raised our kids.
We've since moved on, but that house will always be home to me.

Let no debt remain outstanding,
except the continuing debt to love one another,
for whoever loves others has fulfilled the law.

—ROMANS 13:8 (NIV)

COVERED BRIDGE

My work isn't bogged down with a lot of training. I never studied art in school, so
I don't know a lot of the traditional rules. I'm not a big believer in color wheels
or complementary hues; I'm okay with using orange with pink or purple with
green. I figure if it's good enough for Mother Nature, it's good enough for me!

Love each other with genuine affection,
and take delight in honoring each other.

—ROMANS 12:10 (NLT)

SLEIGH RIDE

Growing up in South Carolina, we didn't see a lot of snow. When we did, though,
it was a party! Schools closed and everyone bundled up and went outside to play.
I have to say, snow still has that effect on me. A sleigh ride is my idea of heaven.

I have set my rainbow in the clouds, and it will be the sign of the covenant between me and the earth.

—GENESIS 9:13 (NIV)

TWO BY TWO

I've noticed that most depictions of Noah's Ark feature elephants, giraffes, monkeys, and such, but there's something grounding about pigs, horses, and cattle. I find that farm animals bring the story about the ark home.

She will give birth to a son
and you are to give him the name Jesus,
because he will save his people from their sins.

—Matthew 1:21 (NIV)

A STAR SHALL GUIDE US

This nativity angel has a special place in my heart. It was an image that came to me fully
formed in an instant, where all the elements seemed to work together just right. If I were
asked to show a single item that best exemplifies my art . . . she might be the one.

Everything that slows us down and forces patience, everything that sets us back into the slow circles of nature, is a help. Gardening is an instrument of grace.

—MAY SARTON

GARDEN GATE

My style is a mix of different folk-art traditions. I use quilt patterns I learned from my grandmother that still inspire me to this day, and then combine those with my own versions of rosemaling and the design style known as Pennsylvania Dutch. It's a synthesis I find exciting, and a combination that energizes my art.

What greater gift than the love of a cat?

—Charles Dickens

LUCKY

A while back, our dog found a stray kitten somewhere out in the woods, wounded
and starving. He brought it home and laid it on our porch. That poor cat was
barely hanging on, but we made it our business to keep him alive. It worked!
We had him for over 15 years, and I've been a cat person ever since.

Now may the Lord of peace himself give you
peace at all times and in every way.
The Lord be with all of you.

—2 Thessalonians 3:16 (NIV)

IN FINE FEATHER

There are a lot of fun facts about cardinals that make them so special. Cardinals mate
for life, so they exemplify loyalty. They don't migrate like other birds, which makes them
homebodies. And they like us! Cardinals live and thrive in trees, shrubs, parks, and yards.
No wonder they're America's favorite bird; the cardinal is the official bird of eight states!

But the fruit of the Spirit is love, joy, peace,
forbearance, kindness, goodness, faithfulness, gentleness,
and self-control. Against such things there is no law.

—Galatians 5:22–23 (NIV)

FAITH AND HARMONY
There aren't many images that I find more soothing than the lion and the lamb.
Its promise of peace always seems to slow the heart and restore the spirit.

Faith is to believe what you do not yet see;
the reward for this faith is to see what you believe.

—St. Augustine

AND NOAH DID ALL THAT THE LORD COMMANDED HIM

One of my great temptations over the years was a desire to include a pair of unicorns
or Bigfoots (or is that Bigfeet?) or some such mythical beast in one of my Noah's Ark
designs. I'm proud to say I've resisted thus far! But I'm thinking there's still time . . .

Trust in the Lord always,
for the Lord God is the eternal Rock.

—Isaiah 26:4 (NLT)

QUIET MOMENT OF BEAUTY

One morning when I was a small boy, my dad called me over to look out the
kitchen window. Outside, not more than five feet from where we stood, was a
brilliant red cardinal perched on a branch. It was a quiet moment of beauty we
shared, just the two of us, and a treasured memory I'll never forget.